# Australian Slang

## A Dictionary

3rd Edition

David Tuffley

To my beloved Nation of Four
*Concordia Domi – Foris Pax*

*As a work of art, it reminds me*
*of a long conversation between two drunks*
*- Clive James*

**3rd Edition Published 2014 by Altiora Publications**
AltioraPublications.com/
**ISBN-13: 978-1477536803 ISBN-10: 1477536809**



**Cover Art by DoublePDesign**
www.doublepdesign.com.au

**About the Author**

David Tuffley is a fourth generation Australian. That makes him a "Dinki di Aussie". His Great Grandfather Henry Tuffley left the Leicestershire village of Hoby in the 1860's, to travel to far-off Australia on a dangerous sea voyage lasting several months. He eventually settled in Cooktown in Far North Queensland where he lived to a ripe old age. Facebook: www.facebook.com/tuffley/

**Acknowledgements**

My brother Steve, my father Alex and the hundreds of people I knew growing up in Cannon Hill, Brisbane. I particularly want to acknowledge the old soldiers who had returned battered and bruised from World War II and the older soldiers who had served in WWI. Also the stalwart wives and mothers who were the real glue of that society regardless of how irascible their men were. These men and women, now mostly gone, were the real repositories of Aussie Slang.

# Introduction

Welcome to Australian Slang, a richly-textured, often ribald world of understatement and laconic humour. This dictionary aims to do three things; (a) help the traveller decipher what they hear around them in everyday Australian life, (b) give the casual reader some insight into informal Australian culture, and (c) make a record of some old Australian expressions that are slipping into disuse now that English has become a global language.

Readers will recognize both British and American terms in this list. Australian English has absorbed much from these two great languages.

For depth of knowledge of their own language, nobody beats the British. They invented the language after all. From its origins as a West Germanic dialect and a thousand years in the making, English is the very soul of what it is to be British. No-one understands or uses their language more skilfully than they do.

Across the Atlantic Ocean, American English had acquired a creative power that recognizes no boundaries. Americans have taken a good all-purpose language and extended it in many directions to describe the world as it is today. They do not cling to old forms out of respect for tradition as the British do. Winston Churchill wryly observed that *Britain and*

*America (are) two great nations divided by the same language.*

Australian English has gone its own way. Take a European language; leave it out in the baking sun and driving rain for a couple of centuries and you have something tough and beautiful, like weathered wood. It is a language that is as much an expression of an ancient landscape as it is a dialect of the early British and Germans who came to live in Australia.

# Origins of Australian English

Australian English began in the early days of settlement as English English with a healthy dash of Celtic influence from the many Scots, Irish and Welsh settlers who came to Australia. Large numbers of German settlers also came in the 1800's, and their influence on the language is also clearly evident.

For over a hundred years, Australia developed in splendid isolation its unique blend of English, tempered by the hardships of heat and cold, deluge and drought, bushfires and cyclones. The harsh environment united people in a common struggle to survive. People helped each other. Strong communitarian loyalties were engendered. It is from this that the egalitarian character of Australia evolved. There is a strong emphasis on building a feeling of solidarity with others. Strangers will call each other "mate" or "luv" in a tone of voice ordinarily reserved for close friends and family in other parts of the world.

Everyone was from somewhere else, and no-one was better than anyone else. A strong anti-authoritarian attitude became deeply embedded in Australian English. This was mainly directed towards their British overlords who still ran the country as a profitable colony.

The Australian sense of humour is generally understated, delivered with a straight-face, and is often self-deprecating in nature. No-one wants to appear to be "up themselves". Harsh or otherwise adverse conditions had to be met without complaint, so when discussing such conditions, it was necessary to do so with laconic, understated humour. Anyone not doing so was deemed a "whinger" (win-jer).

Following World War II the American influence came increasingly to influence Australian culture and therefore the language. No-one is better at selling their popular culture to the world than the United States of America. Their pop culture is a beguiling instrument of foreign policy, so pervasive and persuasive it is. Young Australians enthusiastically embraced American culture, and since the 1940's the old established British language and customs have become blended with the American.

If Australian English has a remarkable quality, it is the absence of regional dialects. It is spoken with relative uniformity across the entire nation. Brisbane on the East coast is a 4,300 kilometre (2,700 mile) drive from Perth on the West coast, yet there is little discernable linguistic difference between the two places compared with the difference, for example between Boston and San Francisco in the US. It is true that the people of steamy Far North Queensland speak a little more slowly than those in chilly Melbourne, nearly 3,000 kilometres to the South, but the difference is not a large one. Nowhere else in the world do we see such linguistic uniformity across large distances.

## The Australian accent

The Australian accent derives from several influences; the East London dialect of English spoken by many of the early convicts, as well as the Irish, Scottish, Welsh and other English accents all had their influence.

Australian's call each other "mate" in the same way that cockney Londoners do. It is a general purpose form of address that can be used with friends, acquaintances and complete strangers alike. It simply indicates a more or less benign attitude toward the other.

While it is fading out with the onset of a flood of American expressions, until recently it was common among working class Australians to use rhyming slang similar to cockney rhyming slang, but with a uniquely

Australian flavour, for example 'let have a butcher's hook' or 'have a Captain Cook' (both meaning to have a look), 'have a dig in the grave' (to shave), and 'on my pat malone' (to be alone).

Another point of similarity between the Australian and Cockney accent is the tendency to pronounce the 'th' sound as 'vv' or 'ff' as in 'farver' for 'father', or 'ffursday' for 'thursday'.

It is also interesting to note that the Canadian accent was influenced by Scottish émigrés, the US accent from the Irish, and the South African accent from the Dutch Afrikaans.

# A

***Ace***: very good, excellent, tops, as in "yeah mate, that was ace".

***After Darks***: rhyming slang for sharks, as in "wouldn't go in there mate, the after darks might get ya".

***Aggro***: being aggressive, looking for a fight or trouble, as in "dunno what's the matter with him, he acting a bit aggro".

***Aerial Ping-Pong***: ARL (Australian Rules League) Football.

***Akubra***: proprietary brand of broad-brimmed felt hat reminiscent of American cowboy hat.

***Al Capone***: rhyming slang for phone.

***Alkie***: alcohol, or a person who is an alcoholic.

***Alice, the***: Alice Springs, an iconic town near the geographic centre of Australia. Named after Lady Alice Todd, wife of Sir Charles who established the telegraph link between Adelaide and the world.

***Almond Rocks***: rhyming slang for socks, as in "oi, have you seen my almond rocks, I left 'em here to dry".

***Amber fluid***: beer.

***Amber Nectar***: beer, as in "I'm quite partial to a drop of the amber nectar".

***Ambo***: an Ambulance or ambulance officer.

***Ammo***: Ammunition.

***Anchors, hit the ...***: apply a vehicle's brakes, particularly in an emergency, as in "I was flyin' along when this roo jumped out, had to hit the anchors real hard".

***Angora Goat***: rhyming slang for throat.

***Ankle-biter***: a small child or crawling infant, particularly one that pesters, as in "how many ankle-biters did you say you had?"

***Any tic of the clock***: any moment now, as in "the trains late, should be here any tick of the clock".

***ANZAC Biscuit***: a popular long-life biscuit first made for WW1 troops from oats and syrup.

***A.N.Z.A.C.***: Australian & New Zealand Army Corps. Joint operations force.

***Apples and Pears***: rhyming slang for stairs.

***Apples***: OK, alright, as in "she'll be apples mate".

***Aristotle***: rhyming slang for bottle.

***Arse***: a person's buttocks.

***Arse Over Tit***: to fall over, particularly in spectacular fashion, as in "should've seen him, went arse over tit down the stairs, silly bugger".

***Arvo***: the Afternoon, as in "what're doing this arvo".

***Ashtray on a surfboard***: a completely useless or impractical thing, as in "it's about as useful as an ashtray on a surfboard (or motorbike)".

***Aussie***: an Australian.

***Aussie Battler***: working class Australian struggling to survive.

***Aussie Salute***: a laconic gesture of waving away flies from around the face.

***Av-a-go-yer-mug***: an exhortation to give something a try, such as one might hear at a sporting contest.

***Awning over the toy shop***: a man's large pot belly/beer gut.

# B

***B & S Ball***: Bachelor's & Spinster's Ball, a tradition in rural Australia where single men and women gather for a night of alcohol-fuelled merriment, as in "I met my missus at the B&S".

***Babbling Brook***: rhyming slang for cook.

***Baccy***: Tobacco, particularly loose leaf for rolling one's own cigarette, as in "you wouldn't have some spare baccy would you?".

***Back of Bourke***: generic term for a location in the Outback, named after town in far northern New South Wales, as in "didn't know where I was, somewhere out back of Bourke".

***Back teeth floating***: a dire need to urinate.

***Bad Case of the Trots***: diarrhoea, particularly due to food poisoning or excessive drinking, as in "not eating that again, gave me a bad case of the trots".

***Bag of Fruit***: rhyming slang for suit, as in "dressed up in my best bag of fruit".

***Bail***: to depart, as in bail out, particularly when a better option presents, as in "he's not here, he bailed on us".

***Banana-Benders***: a Queenslander.

***Bangers***: Australian sausages, similar to English or German sausages for frying.

***Barbie***: barbecue or B.B.Q, as in "you want to come over for a barbie on Saturday?"

***Barney***: a fight, as in "did you see the barney down the pub last night?".

***Barra***: a delicacy, the Barramundi fish from the mangrove-lined estuaries of far northern Australia.

***Barrack***: to cheer or otherwise encourage a sporting team.

***Bastard***: a term of endearment between friends, as in "come on, ya silly old bastard".

***Bathers***: swimming costume, also known as trunks, togs or cossy.

***Battler***: poor or under-privileged person.

***Bean counter***: accountant, as in "it's not been the same since the bean-counters took over".

***Beanie***: a snug fitting knitted woollen cap for keeping the head warm.

***Beaut***: beautiful, as in "that's a beaut-looking fish".

***Bee's Knees***: vey good, as in "he thinks he's the bee's knees".

***Berk***: a foolish person. As in "get off it, yer berk".

***Betcha***: short for "I bet you" as in a wager.

***Big bickies***: big money, as in "you get to decide (on a difficult decision), that's why they pay you the big bickies".

***Big-Note***: to self-aggrandise, as in listen to that idiot big note himself".

***Big Smoke***: A big city or town, as in "won't see you no more, moving to the big smoke".

***Bikey***: Motorcycle rider.

***Bickie***: a biscuit.

***Billabong***: a freshwater pond, often in a half dry river or orphaned river bend, as in "there's bugger-all water in the billabong, you might have to dig for it."

***Billy***: (a) metal cooking vessel used to heat water for tea over an open fire; (b) a cone-like receptacle for smoking cannabis through a pipe or bong.

***Billy Lid***: rhyming slang for kid.

***Bingle***: a usually non-serious collision between motor vehicles, as in "got held up on the way home, there was bingle".

***Bitzer***: a dog of indeterminate mixed breed, as in "a bit of this and a bit of that".

***Boob Tube***: a tube top, an elasticised strapless, tube-shaped garment worn by women on a hot day to display their assets to good effect, as in "check out that girl in the boob-tube".

***Brothel***: (a) a place where sex may be purchased, (b) a mess, as in "Jeez, the place was a brothel after the burglars went through".

***Bities***: generic term for biting insects and arachnids, as in "had to get out of there, too many bities".

***Bitser***: as in Bitzer, a dog of mixed breed.

***Blackfella***: an Australian aboriginal, as in "that's blackfella country".

***Black Stump***: in indeterminate place in the Outback, as in "where is it? dunno, out past the black stump".

***Bloke***: a man, as in "he's a good bloke".

***Blood Blister***: rhyming slang for sister.

***Bloody Oath***: sometimes shortened to Blood Oath, vowing on the truth of a statement, as in "bloody oath I did!".

***Blotto***: very drunk, unconsciously drunk, as in "poor old Jim, totally blotto".

***Blow-in***: a person new on the scene, a recent arrival, as opposed to "a local", as in "we were doing alright until all these blow-ins arrived".

***Blow in the bag***: The command given by Police to test for driving under the influence of alcohol. Bags have long since been replaced with blow-through devices.

***Blowie***: a blow-fly, a species of large fly often found near rotting meat, as in "there were so many blowies on the carcass I thought they were gonna carry it away".

***Bludger***: a lazy or parasitic person, as in "that bludger wouldn't work in an iron-lung".

***Blue***: (a) an argument, often violent; (b) an error, (c) a red-haired man.

***Bluey***: (a) a red-haired man, (b) a blue heeler cattle dog, (c) marine stinger.

***Bodgy***: poor quality work, sometimes dangerously so.

***Bogan***: (a) a rude or uncultured person, (b) a person coming from a low socio-economic suburb or town.

***Bog in***: the signal to begin eating.

***Bong***: a water pipe for smoking cannabis, usually improvised from a drink container and garden hose.

***Bogged***: when a vehicle is immobilised in sand or mud.

***Boofhead***: a loud but relatively harmless oaf.

***Boomerang***: a curved throwing stick used by the indigenous Australians to hunt kangaroos, emus and other large, fast moving animals.

***Bondi Cigar***: floating human faeces encountered while swimming.

***Bonza***: very good, excellent, "that was bonza game".

***Bottle-o***: when empty glass bottles could still be redeemed for money, he went about the neighbourhood proclaiming his presence with the call "Bottle-o!".

***Bottle Shop***: an off-licence, liquor store where alcoholic drinks could be purchased, as in "I'm going down to the bottle-shop for supplies".

***Boogie Board***: a small surf board ridden by kneeling or lying on it, as in "he's been out there for hours on his boogie board".

***Boomer***: a large, and often aggressive male kangaroo.

***Booze Bus***: a mobile Police station where people testing positive to drink driving are charged.

***Boozer***: a working class establishment primarily for getting drunk in.

***Bored Shitless***: Very bored, as in "there's nothing to do here, I'm bored shitless".

***Brass Razoo***: a very low-value, fictional coin, as in "I'm broke, don't have a brass razoo".

***Bread and Jam***: rhyming slang for tram.

***Brekkie***: breakfast, as in "what's for brekkie?".

***Brick Shit House***: a structure or person that is of very solid build, as in "don't mess with that bloke, he's built like a brick shithouse".

***Brickie***: Bricklayer in the construction industry, as in "do you know a good brickie I could get in (to do a job for me)"?

***Brizzie***: Brisbane capital of Queensland.

***Briz-Vegas***: derogatory name given to Brisbane by Sydney and Melbourne people due to it being perceived as having more flash than substance.

***Brown Eyed Mullet***: faeces floating in the water.

***Brown-nose***: an obsequious person, as in "have a look at him, brown-nosing the boss".

***Brumby***: wild horse, similar to a mustang, as in "I nearly hit brumby on the way in".

***Buckley's***: absolutely no chance, as in "he's got buckley's with her".

***Buck's night***: men-only party, often preceding a wedding. Similar to a stag-party.

***Budgie Smugglers***: men's brief swimming trunks, sometimes derisively known as "Dick Togs", which display the man's "package", leaving little to the imagination.

***Bull Bar***: a steel barrier welded to the front of vehicles to protect them from collisions with stray animals on the road.

***Bundy***: (a) Bundaberg Rum, a dark, full-flavoured rum distilled in the Queensland town of Bundaberg, (b) a time clock.

***Bunch of Fives***: a fist.

***Bunyip***: a mythical, yowie/yeti-like creature said to inhabit the Australian bush. Often used to frighten children or gullible visitors.

***Bush***: generic forested country outside of settled areas.

***Bushed***: tired, worn out.

***Bush Bashing***: blazing a trail through the bush, on foot or in a four wheel drive vehicle equipped with a bull-bar.

***Burl***: to attempt something, as in "yeah, I'll give it a burl".

***Bushie***: (a) a person who lives in and understands the Bush, as in "that's old Kev, the bushie", (b) a member of the volunteer fire brigade who fight bush-fires.

***Bushman's Clock***: a kookaburra (a member of the kingfisher family known for its raucous dawn chorus).

***Bushranger***: an outlaw who hides from the law in the bush when not robbing people.

***Bush Telegraph***: the informal social network by which news and gossip spreads, similar to "the grapevine".

***Bush Tucker***: generic term for food found in the Australian bush or outback, as in "he lived on bush tucker for a month until they picked him up".

***Bushwhacker***: a robber who ambushes travellers, similar to Bushranger.

***Bushwalking***: hiking in the great Australian outdoors.

***Bust a gut***: to work very hard, literally to give oneself a hernia, as in "I bust a gut to get that done".

***Buster***: a strong, sometimes destructive wind.

***Butcher's Hook***: rhyming slang for "Look".

***Buzz Off***: to tell someone to go away while comparing them to an insect.

***B.Y.O.***: Bring Your Own (food and/or drinks), as in "come over for a barbie on Saturday, BYO"

# C

*Cabbie*: taxi driver.

*Cactus*: dead, completely spent, finished, as in "the dog is cactus, got hit by a car".

*Cakehole*: a person's mouth, as in "shut your cakehole".

*Call it a day*: finish or call and end to something, as in "think it's time we called it a day".

*Call it Quits*: finish or call and end to something.

*Captain Cook*: rhyming slang for look, as in "I'm going over to have a captain cook".

*Cancer Stick*: a cigarette.

*Carbie*: the carburettor of a motor, as in "she's running a bit rough, I think it's the carbie".

*Cark It*: to die, as in become a carcass, as in "I want to see the pyramids before I cark it".

*Cheerio*: goodbye, farewell.

*Cheese 'n Kisses*: rhyming slang for missus.

*Cheesed Off*: to be very annoyed, as in "to say I'm cheesed off would be an understatement".

*Chemist*: Pharmacist.

***Chew the Fat***: a relaxed, informal, often extended conversation, as in "those blokes would rather sit around and chew the fat than do some actual work".

***Chewie***: chewing gum, as in "damn, stepped in some chewie".

***Chin Wag***: a relaxed, informal conversation, as in "we should catch up for a bit of chin wag".

***Chips***: deep fried potato chips, similar to French fries.

***Chippie***: Carpenter.

***Chockie***: Chocolate, as in "that's bloody good chockie".

***Chook***: generic name for a domestic chicken., as in "go and feed the chooks, will ya".

***Chrissie***: Christmas, as in "what'd you get for Chrissie?"

***Chuck***: to throw an object or a temper-tantrum, as in "chuck us cold one will ya" or "jeez, he chucked a wobbly over that one".

***Chuck Up***: to vomit, as in "he chucked up his lunch on the way over in the boat".

***Chuck a Sickie***: to claim sick-leave when not actually sick, as in "think I'll take a sickie today, weather's too good to go to work".

***Chuck a Spaz***: a tantrum or display of bad temper.

***Chuck a U-ie***: to make a vehicular U-turn, as in "went down the wrong road, had to chuck a u-ie".

***Chuck a Wobbly***: a tantrum or display of bad temper.

***Chunder***: to vomit, as in "watch out under" said by sea-sick mariners to warn people on lower decks.

***Clayton's***: an (often second-rate) substitute for the real thing.

***Cleanskin***: livestock that bears no marks of ownership.

***Clear as mud***: unclear idea or situation, as in "thanks for explaining that, clear as mud".

***Click***: a kilometre, as in "it's about 20 clicks down that way".

***Clobber***: (a) to hit someone hard; (b) clothes, as in "he was wearing his best clobber".

***Clucky***: describing a female who is creating an environment into which babies may safely be brought.

***Coat Hanger***: the iconic Sydney Harbour Bridge.

***Cobber***: friend, partner.

***Cockie***: (a) cockatoo; (b) cockroach; (c) Australian farmer; (d) to behave in a somewhat jaunty or arrogant way.

***Come a Gutser***: to suffer misfortune, often through over-confidence, as in "he was so cockie he was bound to come a gutser sooner or later".

***Comic Cuts***: rhyming slang for guts.

***Compo***: Worker's Compensation, a form of accident insurance paid to workers injured while employed, as in "he's still on compo after the accident".

***Cone***: (a) a traffic control device, sometimes called a witches hat; (b) a cone-shaped pipe for smoking cannabis, as in "I'm going home and havin' a few cones".

***Cooking with Gas***: everything is going well, or very well, as in "yeah mate, its going well, we're cookin' with gas".

***Cooee***: (a) a high-pitched human call that carries long distances in the bush, used to locate one another; (b) in the local area, as "no shops within cooee of here".

***Corroboree***: an indigenous Australian celebration of culture, often involving dancing.

***Cossie**, or **Cozzie***: swim-suit, as in "you can't swim in the nuddy here mate, you gotta wear a cossie".

***Couch Potato***: person who spends so long on the couch watching TV or playing computer games that they begin to sprout roots into the dirt in which they sit.

***Counter Lunch***: lunch at a licensed hotel. Counter lunches are ordered from the bar, and collected when your number is called.

***Country Cousin***: rhyming slang for dozen.

***Crack a Fat***: to achieve an erect penis, as in "she was so hot, I couldn't help but crack a fat".

***Cranky***: ill-tempered.

***Crash***: (a) to spend the night at another's home usually after drinking, (b) to pass out from intoxication, (c) to arrive uninvited at a social gathering.

***Cream*** [verb]: to defeat, as in "we creamed them".

***Crim***: criminal.

***Croc***: (a) nonsense, lies; (b) crocodile.

***Crook***: (a) to feel unwell, as in "I'm feeling bit crook today, go without me", (b) a criminal.

***Crown Jewels***: testicles, as in "the bastard got me in the crown jewels, it was low blow".

***Crows fly backwards***: a remote part of the outback, as in "out where the crows fly backwards". They do this to "keep the dust out of their eyes".

***Cubby House***: a children's playhouse in the garden.

***Cuppa***: cup of tea.

***Curry and Rice***: rhyming slang for price.

***Cut Snake***: to be "mad as a cut snake" to be very angry.

# D

***Dad 'n Dave***: rhyming slang for shave.

***Dag***: a socially inept person, as in "look at him, he's such a dag".

***Daks***: pants worn by men and boys, as in "he fell over and ripped the bum right out of his daks".

***Damper***: simple unleavened bread made in the coals of a camp-fire, a staple of early Australian settlers.

***Date***: a person's anus or buttocks.

***Date Roll***: toilet paper.

***Dead-Cert***: a certainty, as in "that horse is a dead-cert".

***Dead Horse***: tomato sauce, ketchup, as in "you got any dead-horse for this pie?".

***Dead Ringer***: looking exactly the same as another, as in "he was a dead-ringer of his old man".

***Dead Set***: truthfully, as in "dead set mate, I couldn't have done it any better".

***Derro***: derelict, a homeless person, often an alcoholic, as in "what happened to Kev? mate he's a bit of a derro these days".

***Dial***: person's face, as in "that'll put a smile on your dial".

***Dickhead***: a foolish person, often one who allows his sex drive to influence his behaviour, as in "don't be a dickhead all your life".

***Didgeridoo***: an indigenous wind-instrument made from a small hollowed log.

***Digger***: an Australian soldier, or former soldier.

***Dill***: a foolish person, as in "yeah you'd have to say he's a bit of dill".

***Dingo***: (a) Australian wild dog related to the Asiatic Wolf; (b) a cowardly or untrustworthy person.

***Dinkie-Di***: genuine, the real thing, as in "he's a dinky-di bloke".

***Dinkum***: Real and true.

***Dipstick***: a foolish person.

***Divvy Van***: Police van used to transport persons under arrest.

***Doco***: documentary.

***Dob in***: to inform on someone to the authorities, as in "you dob me in and I'll fucking kill ya".

***Dodge and Shirk***: rhyming slang for work.

***Dog***: (a) prison informer; (b) an ugly woman.

***Dog and Bone***: rhyming slang for phone.

***Dog's Balls***: prominently displayed, as in "they stuck out like dog's balls".

***Dogs Breakfast***: a shambles, a mess, as in "the place was like a dog's breakfast when I got home".

***Dog's Eye***: rhyming slang for a meat pie, as in "yeah, I'll get a dog's eye thanks mate".

***Dole Bludger***: a person receiving unemployment benefits who is fit for work but prefers not to, as in "that bloke? he's a dole bludger, hasn't worked in years".

***Dollop***: a serving of food, usually from a ladle, as in "you couldn't give a second dollop, could ya?".

***Donger***: penis, as in "it was as dry as a dead dingoes' donga".

***Donk***: general term for an engine, as in "what kind of donk you got there?".

***Doodle***: (a) penis; (b) free-style drawing.

***Doona***: a duvet or down-filled quilted bed-spread, as in "jeez luv, don't hog all the doona".

***Down Under***: in relation to Britain, Australia is down under on the globe.

***Drongo***: a slow witted or foolish person.

***Drain the dragon***: to urinate, as in "goin' outside, gotta drain the dragon (or syphon the python)".

***Drive a nail into a bucket of water***: an incompetent driver, as in "he couldn't drive a nail ...".

***Drop Bear***: a mythical tree-dwelling bear that drops out of trees to prey on people. Used to frighten gullible visitors.

***Drover's breakfast***: literally a drink of water and a look around, meaning to start the day without breakfast.

***Drum***: tip-off, as in "I'll give you the drum, don't go there mate".

***Dry as a wooden god***: see Wooden god.

***Ducks 'n Geese***: rhyming slang for police.

***Dud***: a non-functioning or otherwise useless person or thing.

***Duds***: man's pants.

***Duffer***: (a) a foolish but lovable person, (b) a cattle thief.

***Dunny***: outdoor toilet or privvy, often merely a hole in the ground, also known as a "thunder-box".

***Durrie***: a cigarette, often a roll-your-own, as in "hey mate, got a spare durrie?"

# E

***Ear-bashing***: (a) incessant talking; (b) a reprimand.

***Eat the horse and chase the rider***: extremely hungry, as in "I'm so hungry, I could eat the horse ...".

***Eating with the flies***: solo dining.

***Egg On***: urge a person to do something they are reluctant to do.

***Elbow Grease***: hard manual labour, particularly involving rubbing or scrubbing, as in “this car's seen better days, but with some elbow-grease, she'll be right as rain”.

***Entree***: first course of a multi-course meal.

***Esky***: insulted, portable cooler box, as in “grab me a beer from the esky will ya”.

# F

***Face fungus***: stubble or whiskers, particularly when a man is sporting an unconvincing bear, as in "what's with the face fungus?".

***Fag***: a cigarette, as in “can you spare a fag?”.

***Fair Dinkum***: truthful, down-to-earth, and reliable, as in “fair dinkum mate, it’s an out and out disgrace”.

***Fairy Floss***: spun sugar confection similar to candy floss.

***Fair Crack of the Whip***: an appeal for as equal a chance as anyone else gets, as in “fair crack of the whip, I just want what’s mine”.

***Fair Go***: an appeal for an equal chance as anyone else, as in “fair go mate, it was broken when I got here”.

***Fair Suck of the Sav***: variant on the appeal for fair go (see preceding).

***Fang - It***: to drive very fast, as in “I had to really fang-it to get here in time”.

***Fanny***: female genitals.

***FITH syndrome***: stupidity, an acronym for "fucked in the head".

*Five Finger Discount*: to steal from a shop, the proceeds of shop-lifting.

*Fix your Jack and Jill*: pay the bill.

*Flake*: (a) an unreliable person, (b) shark meat as sold over the counter.

*Flat out like a lizard drinking*: being very busy, working hard, as in "dead set mate, I've been working flat out like a lizard drinking".

*Flick*: (a) to discard an unwanted item, as in "give him the flick"; (b) pass it on, as in "flick that over to me".

*Flog*: (a) to sell goods or services; (b) physically beat a person or animal, (c) engage in a futile attempt, as in "you're flogging a dead-horse there mate".

*Fossick*: to search for something, especially for gemstones and precious metals.

*Footie*: generic term for football in Australia, either Australian Rules (derived from Irish Gaelic football), or Rugby Union (from English Public Schools) or Rugby League (an Australian variant on Rugby Union). Ironically, does not include soccer which is played almost exclusively with the feet.

*Forgive and Forget*: rhyming slang for cigarette.

*Fred Nerk*: a generic man's name, any man in the street.

*Fridge*: refrigerator.

*Frog and Toad*: rhyming slang for road, as in "gotta hit the frog and toad".

***Froth and Bubble:*** rhyming slang for trouble.

***Fruit Loop***: a person of unsound mind, as in "don't ask him, he's fruit-loop".

***Full as a Boot***: to be fully sated, having had one's fill of food and/or drink.

***Full as a Goog***: drunk, intoxicated, particularly when behaving comically, as in full as an egg.

***Furphy***: an unreliable rumour.

# G

*Gabba*: the Brisbane Cricket Ground at Wooloongabba, as in "Australia v England, this weekend at the Gabba".

*G'day*: general purpose informal greeting, pronounced "Gidday" with flattened vowel sounds, not "Goodday".

*Galah*: a noisy and/or foolish person, as in "ya silly galah".

*Gander*: To have a look, a squiz, a peek, as in "have a gander at this".

*Garbo*: garage collector.

*Georgie Moore:* rhyming slang for door.

*German Band*: rhyming slang for hand.

*Germaine Greer*: rhyming slang for ear.

*Gibber Jabber*: nonsensical speech, as in "what kind of jibber-jabber is that?".

*Ginger Beer*: rhyming slang for ear.

*Ginger Meggs*: rhyming slang for legs.

*Gin Sling*: rhyming slang for ring.

***Give It A Burl***: to try something, even though the outcome is uncertain, as in "yeah I might give it a burl, see what happens".

***Gizmo***: general purpose name for a technological artefact.

***Gobful***: a barrage of abuse, as in "man, did he give me gobful for chatting to his missus".

***Gobsmacked***: to be speechless with surprise.

***Good-on-yer-mate***: general purpose statement indicating approval or good intent.

***Good Nick***: good condition, as in "the car has 150k on the clock, but she's still in good nick".

***Good Oil***: the real truth, as opposed to what people might want you to think, as in "I'll give you the good oil on race 4".

***Good On-ya***: as with good on-yer mate, above..

***Gregory Peck***: rhyming slang for neck.

***Greenie***: environmentalist or ecologist.

***Grim and Gory***: rhyming slang for story.

***Grog***: alcoholic drink, especially strong drink like rum or bourbon, as in "where's jim? he's on the grog".

***Grouse***: (a) very good, as "she's a grouse sheila (woman)", (b) a brand of Scotch Whisky The Famous Grouse, as in "give us a double grouse".

***Grot***: a dirty and or dingy space, as in a grotto, as in "it's not a bad place, shame it's a bit grotty".

***Gurgler***: the drain hole leading down into the sewer, as in "mate, his chances are down the gurgler".

***Grundies***: a man's underpants, variant on "under-grundy".

***Gyno***: gynaecologist

# H

***Hair of the Dog***: hangover remedy involving more alcohol, as in "I felt a bit rough when I woke up, bit a hair of the dog fixed that".

***Half Your Luck***: you are so lucky that if I had half your luck, I'd be happy.

***Ham and Eggs***: rhyming slang for legs.

***Handle***: a person's name.

***Hang On***: request to wait a short time, as in "yeah, hang-on a sec".

***Happy as a pig in mud***: to enjoy oneself, particular when mess-making is involved.

***Hard Yakka***: hard, often prolonged labour, as in "digging that trench was hard yakka".

***Heaps***: ample, more than enough, as in "love ya heaps".

***Heart-starter***: the first alcoholic drink for the day, often consumed at breakfast, as in "you want a heart starter with those eggs?".

***Heave***: vomit.

***His Nibs***: the person in command, as in "look out, here comes his nibs".

***Hoof***: a person's foot.

***Hoof It***: to travel on foot, as in "ran out of petrol so I had to hoof it".

***Hoon***: person who drives fast, hard and dangerously.

***Hoo-roo***: good-bye.

***Hotel***: premises licensed to sell alcoholic drinks.

# I

***Icy Pole***: an ice confection with a wooden stick embedded in one end as a handle.

***Idiot Box***: television.

***I Kid You Not***: I'm telling you the truth.

***In the Altogether***: to be nude.

***In the Nuddie***: to be nude.

***In the Shit***: to be in serious trouble or difficulty.

# J

***Jack and Jill:*** rhyming slang for bill.

***Jack Jones:*** rhyming slang for bones.

***Jackaroo***: mounted (on horse or motor bike) stockman who musters cattle and performs general duties on the cattle station.

***Jam Tart:*** rhyming slang for heart.

***Jelly***: a gelatine-based confection.

***Jiffy***: soon.

***Jillaroo***: female equivalent of jackeroo, as above.

***Jimmy Grant:*** rhyming slang for immigrant.

***Joe Blake:*** rhyming slang for snake.

***John Hop:*** rhyming slang for cop.

***Johnny Horner:*** rhyming slang for corner.

***Joe Baxi:*** rhyming slang for taxi.

***Joe Bloggs***: generic name, similar to John Doe.

***Joey***: immature kangaroo or wallaby, often still being carried in mother's pouch.

***Journo***: journalist, as in "he's a journo working for Murdoch".

***Jug***: electric kettle, as in "whack the jug on for a cuppa".

***Jumbuck***: a sheep.

# K

***Kangaroo***: member of the marsupial genus Macropus, bi-pedal native of Australia and no-where else. Members of this diverse genus range from small, cat-sized paddy-melons up to two meter tall "big red" kangaroos living in the remote outback.

***Kark it***: to die, to become a carcass, as in "he was lost out there for week – karked it".

***Kelpie***: a tough and versatile working dog for sheep or cattle mustering.

***Kero***: kerosene, or paraffin.

***Kick the Bucket***: to die, as in "he was only 27 when he kicked the bucket".

***Kindie***: kindergarten, a child-minding centre for pre-school age children.

***Kip***: a short nap, or siesta.

***Kitchen Sink***: rhyming slang for drink.

***Kiwi***: New Zealander.

***Knee High to a Grasshopper***: a young child, as in "I've known Bluey since he was knee-high to a grasshopper".

***Knock***: to criticise or disparage, as in "don't knock it until you try it".

***Knock Back***: a refusal, when someone declines an offer, particularly when done gracelessly, as in "I tried to join the team but they knocked me back".

***Knocker***: one who criticises or disparages, as in "the knockers had a field day".

***Knuckle Sandwich***: a punch in the mouth, as in "mind your manners or you'll get a knuckle sandwich".

# L

***Lair***: a show-off, a flashy dresser, as in "that's flash harry, the mug lair".

***Lamington***: small sponge cakes covered in chocolate icing and rolled in coconut.

***Larrikin***: a happy-go-lucky, sometimes mischievous person.

***Lay By***: to purchase something on an instalment plan.

***Lead Foot***: a fast and often reckless driver.

***Legend***: a person of heroic accomplishments, as in "that bloke's a legend".

***Lend Of***: to take advantage of a trusting person.

***Lino***: linoleum, the floor covering.

***Lionel Rose***: rhyming slang for nose. Lionel Rose was an indigenous boxing champion.

***Lippie/lippy***: lipstick.

***Liquid Laugh***: vomit.

***Lob in***: arrive unannounced.

***Local Rag***: local newspaper.

***Lower than a snake's armpit***: an underhanded or despicable act.

***Lollipop Lady or Man***: school crossing supervisor, as in "the mad bugger nearly ran over the lollipop lady".

***Lolly***: (a) candy, confectionary of any kind; (b) money.

***Lolly Water***: soft drink, soda pop.

***London to a Brick***: absolute certainty.

***Longneck***: 750ml bottle of beer, esp. in South Australia.

***Long Paddock***: the grassy strip beside roads where livestock might graze. In time of drought, the long paddock provided much needed fodder.

***Loo***: toilet, as in "I'm just going to the loo".

***Lubra***: indigenous woman or girl.

***Lucky Country***: Australia.

***Lurk***: a scheme of questionable legality or ethics.

# M

*Macca's*: McDonald's, the fast food franchise, as in "I've got the munchies, let's go down to Maccas".

*Mad as a cut snake*: very angry, as in "I'd steer clear, he's as mad as a cut snake".

*Mad Mike*: rhyming slang for push bike.

*Make a Quid*: how a person makes their living.

*Make Do*: improvise with what is available.

*Malley Bull*: a feral bull living in the scrub country of remote regional Australia. Such bulls are fearsome creatures. To be compared to one is a compliment. It is to be fit and strong and ready for action, as in "he's as fit as a malley bull".

*Malvern Star*: rhyming slang for car.

*Marble orchard*: cemetery, as in "pushing up daisy's in the marble orchard".

*Mate*: a general purpose term of address indicating good will and solidarity for the addressee. Derives directly from the East London term and has the same meaning.

*Mate's Rates*: discounted price for a friend.

***Manchester***: generic term for household linen. Department stores still have a "Manchester" department. Derives from the city in England where linen was first produced and exported to the world.

***Mary Lee***: rhyming slang for tea.

***Matilda***: a travelling man's sleeping roll, often carried rolled up and slung across his back. Also known as a "swag".

***Metho***: denatured alcohol or methylated spirits. Made from ethanol but with additives to make it poisonous and foul-asting to discourage consumption. Metho is still consumed by some hard-core alcoholics despite the toxic, blinding effect of the methanol that the manufacturers add to deter consumption.

***Middy***: in New South Wales, a middy is a 285 ml or 10oz. glass of beer.

***Milk Bar***: local convenience store selling milk, bread, cigarettes. These local corner stores have largely disappeared from suburban Australia since planning regulations now require off-street parking for multiple cars, which the old style stores are unable to provide.

***Milko***: the milkman who delivers fresh milk to the door.

***Mob***: (a) a group of people; (b) a group of kangaroos; (c) a flock of sheep.

***Mollycoddle***: to spoil a child through not exposing them to the harsh realities of life, as in "don't mollycoddle the boy!".

*Molly the Monk*: rhyming slang for drunk.

***Mongrel***: (a) a dog of mixed or indeterminate breed, (b) a contemptible person.

***Moolah***: money, especially cash money.

***More arse than class***: a high achievement that is put down to luck, not skill, as in "yeah they won on Saturday, but it was more arse than class".

*Mozzie*: mosquito.

***Mucking Around***: aimless play or experimentation, as in "oi you lot, stop your mucking around".

*Mud Pies*: rhyming slang for eyes.

***Muddy***: mud crab, a delicacy for the table.

***Mug***: (a) general purpose term of abuse; (b) a gullible person.

***Mulga***: an Acacia tree that grows across thousands of square miles of Outback Australia.

***Munchies:*** being irrepressibly hungry, often as a result of smoking cannabis.

***Mull***: cannabis leaf prepared for smoking, often blended with tobacco or hashish.

***Muster***: to gather a herd of sheep or cattle together for some purpose (eg branding, inoculation, transportation to market).

*Mutt and Jeff*: rhyming slang for deaf.

***Mystery Bags***: Sausages, so named because offal is sometimes used as a bulking agent.

# N

*Nasho*: conscription into the military, as in National Service, discontinued in Australia in the 1970's at the end of the Viet Nam war.

*Nappy*: diaper.

*Nail and Screws*: rhyming slang for news.

*Naughty*: recreational sex, as in "have got time for a naughty?".

*Near and Far*: rhyming slang for bar.

*Ned Kelly*: rhyming slang for belly.

*Nellie Bligh*: rhyming slang for fly.

*Nelly McGuire*: rhyming slang for light the fire.

*Never Never*: (a) the remote Outback; (b) to buy something on credit, as in you will never end up paying it off. ]

*New Australian*: newly arrived migrant.

*Nick*: (a) to steal; (b) Police lockup/custody.

*Nick Off*: leave, as in "hey kid, nick off!"

*Nipper*: (a) a junior surf life saver; (b) general term for a child.

*Noah's Ark*: rhyming slang for shark.

*No Worries*: general term indicating (a) agreement; (b) that something is possible; (c) good will.

*No-Hoper*: a low-achieving person whose prospects are deemed to be poor.

*Noodling*: looking for gemstones, particularly opals.

*Not the Full Quid*: a person of below average intelligence, as in "old bill's not the full quid".

*Noggin*: a person's head, particular the top of the head.

*Nong*: a foolish person.

*Nose, on the...*: a disagreeable smell, as in "that cheese is on the nose".

*Nut Out*: to work something out through intellectual effort.

*Nuddy*: in the nude.

# O

***O.S.***: overseas, as in "I'm going OS when I finish uni".

***Ocker***: a vulgar Australian, usually male.

***Off Your Face***: to be incapacitated through drink or other recreational drug, as in "I was off my face, I don't remember anything about it".

***Off the Beaten Track***: (a) the road less travelled; (b) a remote location.

***Off Sider***: an assistant, as in "don't bother me now, give it to me off-sider".

***Old Cheese***: slightly derogatory term for one's mother.

***Old Feller***: penis, as in "so I whacked me old feller out and shoved it in".

***Old Man***: (a) someone's father; (b) a woman's husband.

***Old Woman***: (a) someone's mother, (b) a man's wife.

***Olds or Oldies***: collective term for one's parents.

***One Armed Bandit***: poker machine.

***Op Shop***: opportunity shop, a second hand goods shop, often operated by charities like the Salvation Army, as in "got this jacket at the op shop".

***Open Slather***: a free-for-all, anything goes.

***On for Young and Old***: a riot in which everyone is involved.

***On the Nose***: a bad smell.

***Outback***: general term for in-land Australia. While the coastal fringes of Australia are generally well-watered and fertile, the vast majority of in-land Australia is dry, ranging from grasslands to acacia scrub to barren desert the further one goes towards the geographic centre of the continent.

***Out in the Sticks***: a remote location, usually somewhere in the Outback.

***Outhouse***: an outside toilet, often a telephone booth-sized building.

***Oxford Scholar***: rhyming slang for dollar.

***Oz***: abbreviated name for Australia, suggestive of it being a mythical place as in the Wizard of Oz.

# P

***Pack a Wallop***: a substantial impact, (a) punch; (b) alcohol/drug, as in "jeez, whatever's in that packs a punch!".

***Package***: a man's genitals as seen through "Budgie Smuggler" swimming trunks, or lycra athletic wear.

***Paddock***: a fenced pasture for grazing livestock.

***Pash***: to kiss passionately, as in "they were pashing at the dance, who knows what happened later".

***Pat Malone***: rhyming slang for alone, as in "nah mate, no-one else is here, I'm on me pat malone".

***Pav***: a pavlova desert, made from baked egg-white and castor sugar, as in "can you bring a dessert to the barbie, something like a pav'd be good".

***Perve***: (a) a pervert, sexual deviant, (b) to lustfully look at someone, as in "there's always gonna be some perves down at the nude beach".

***Pictures***: the cinema.

***Piece of Piss***: can be accomplished with ease, as in "it'll be easy, piece of piss".

***Pig's arse!***: a derisive denial of another's assertion, as in "pig's arse you didn't do it, I saw ya!".

***Pinch***: (a) to steal; (b) to nip someone's skin between forefinger and thumb.

***Piss***: (a) general term for alcoholic drink, as in "he's been on the piss since saturday".; (b) to urinate.

***Pissing in your pocket***: telling a misleading story, as in "I'm not pissin' in your pocket, it happened just like that".

***Plant Your Foot***: put your foot down hard on a vehicle's accelerator, as in "mate, we're running late; put your foot down!".

***Plate, bring a***: an informal gathering where everyone brings food to share, as in "a few of us are getting together, you wanna come? Yeah, just bring a plate".

***Plates of Meat***: rhyming slang for feet, as in "look at the size of those plates of meat, he's got a good grip on the planet".

***Plodder***: a slow but often effective worker. , as in "jim's alright, bit of plodder, but he gets the job done".

***Plonk***: cheap alcoholic drink, usually wine. , as in "g'day mate, what've you got there, your usual plonk?".

***Pokies***: poker machines, as in "Mum's down playing the pokies (at the local pub/club)". Also known as "One Armed Bandits".

***Polish Off***: to quickly consume something, as in "jeez, he polished off that pizza".

***Polly***: politician.

***Pom, Pommy, Pommie***: Englishman.

***Poofter***: derogatory name for male homosexual.

***Poofter Basher***: a violent homophobe.

***Porkie***: a lie, derived from Cockney English "Pork Pie".

***Pork Pie***: rhyming slang for lie.

***Port***: valise or suitcase.

***Postie***: mailman.

***Pot***: (a) cannabis; (b) a 285 ml Beer Glass.

***Pozzie***: position, as in "you have a great pozzie there mate".

***Prang***: a road traffic accident, as in "phew, saw a nasty prang on the way home".

***Prawn***: crustacean known elsewhere as shrimp, as in "man I could eat these prawns till I burst".

***Prezzy***: a present, as in "thanks for the prezzy".

***Pub***: public house, hotel.

***Puffed***: out of breath, exhausted.

***Push Bike***: bicycle

# Q

***QANTAS***: acronym of Australia's national airline (Queensland and Northern Territory Aerial Service). Now headquartered in Sydney, the airline was founded in 1920 and based in Winton, Western Queensland.

***Quack***: medical practitioner, particularly one of questionable competence, as in "you better go see the quack about that rash".

***Quid***: informal name for the old imperial currency based on the British Pound (£). Australia moved to decimal currency ($) in 1966.

***Quid** - **make a***: make money.

***Quid** - **not the full***: a person of below average intelligence, as in "yeah, don't worry about him, he's not the full quid".

***Quilt***: bed-clothes, particularly the top-most layer.

# R

***RSL Club***: Returned Services League Club, a social club with branches across Australia for serving and retired members of the Australian military and their guests.

***Rack Off***: go away, as "rack-off hairy legs!".

***Rag***: local newspaper, as in "yeah, I saw it in the local rag".

***Rage***: an exciting party or social gathering.

***Ratbag***: a scoundrel.

***Rat-shit***: (a) feeling unwell; (b) general expression for not good. Sometimes abbreviated to RS.

***Raw Prawn***: to attempt to hood-wink a person, as in "don't come the raw prawn with me, son".

***Razoo***: fictitious brass coin of low value.

*RC*: Roman Catholic, with the double entendre that Catholics are remotely controlled.

***Reffo***: a refugee, as in "there's too many reffos coming here on boats".

***Rego***: government tax on motor vehicles to allow them to drive on publicly funded roads, from "Registration".

***Rellies***: a person's relatives, their extended family, as in "yeah, we got the rellies coming for Christmas".

***Ridgy-didge***: honestly, truthfully.

***Ring In***: a deceptive substitution, as in "the horse that won the fifth race was definitely a ring-in".

***Rip Snorter***: very good.

***Ripper***: a general statement indicating approval or pleasure, as in "you little ripper!"

***Road Train***: a big rig comprised of a powerful prime mover with up to four trailers. Only operate in remote parts of Australia where the roads are long, straight, and with few bends. Used to transport livestock and occasionally other goods.

***Roadie***: beer you buy to take with you on a journey.

***Rock and Lurch***: rhyming slang for church.

***Rock Up***: to arrive, often unexpectedly, as in "just rock-up anytime".

***Rollie***: roll your own cigarette.

***Ron***: later on, as in "I'll take two, one for me, one for ron".

***Roo***: kangaroo.

***Roo Bar***: similar to bull bar, a welded steel guard mounted on the front of a vehicle to protect against the impact of hitting animals on the highway.

***Roos loose***: screws loose, as in not quite sane; "He's got a few roos loose in the top paddock."

***Root***: to copulate, as in "yeah mate, she's a bloody good root".

***Ropeable***: extremely angry.

***Rory O'Moore**:* rhyming slang for close the door.

***Rort***: a fraudulent scheme.

***Rotten***: very drunk.

***Rough end of the pineapple***: a bad deal.

***Roustabout***: a general support worker in a shearing shed, not a shearer, but the one who fetches and carries.

***Rubber***: (a) a pencil eraser; (b) condom.

***Rubbish***: to denigrate, as in "hey, don't you rubbish my mate!"

# S

***Sack***: bed, as in "I'm gonna hit the sack".

***Sack, to***: to have one's employment terminated, as in "we had to sack him, he was bloody useless".

***Saint Louis Blues***: rhyming slang for shoes.

***Salvo***: member of the Salvation Army, also known as "Sallies".

***Sand Shoes***: sports shoes with canvas uppers and rubber soles .(eg Dunlop Volley tennis shoes).

***Sanger***: sandwich.

***Sausage Roll***: rhyming slang for goal.

***Sav***: saveloy, a processed meat sausage, usually red in colour, used in hot dogs.

***Scallops***: (a) sliced potato, battered and deep fried; (b) edible shell-fish.

***Scarce as Hen's Teeth***: very rare or non-existent.

***Schoolie***: (a) adolescent of school age; (b) person who recently finished their secondary schooling who have embarked on a week-long alcohol fuelled party at a resort destination. If a person has not lost their virginity before schoolies, there is a heightened chance that they will lose it during. "Schoolies" is therefore a rite of passage for many young adults.

***Schooner***: a "schooner" is a 15 oz glass of beer.

***Scorcher***: very hot day, as in "jeez it's a scorcher today, must be up in the high 30's".

***Scratchy***: instant lottery ticket.

***Screamer***: someone who gets drunk on relatively little alcohol, as in "he's a two pot screamer".

***Scrub***: native forest in more marginal areas where the trees are small, little more than large acacia shrubs (eg mulga, or gidyea trees, pronounced *gidgee*)

***Scrub Up***: to get ready for a social event where one wants to look one's best, as in "you scrubbed up well luv".

***Scrubber***: (a) feral cattle that have evaded mustering through having hidden in the scrub; (b) an uncouth woman.

***Seppo***: an American, derived from rhyming slang "Septic Tank".

***Septics Tanks***: an American (see above).

***Servo***: service station, a place to buy fuel for a vehicle.

***Shag on a Rock***: to be very obvious, as in "he stands out in the crowd like a shag on a rock".

***Shark Biscuit***: novice surfer.

***Sheep-Shagger***: A New Zealander

***Sheila***: general term for a female, not derogatory, equivalent of "bloke" for a man.

***She'll be Right***: the situation will resolve itself satisfactorily, as in "go on mate, she'll be right".

***Shingle short***: a not very intelligent person, as in "don't ask him, he's a shingle short on the roof of life".

***Shit House***; (a) toilet; (b) poor quality, as in "this food is shit-house".

***Shonky***: (a) a con man, as in "he's a shonk"; (b) poor quality goods.

***Shoot Through***: to exit a situation, usually without ceremony, as in "this party's dead, think I'll shoot through".

***Shout***: Your turn to buy or purchase a round of drinks, as in "come on, it's your shout".

***Shut Eye***: sleep.

***Sickie***: sick-leave, usually without just cause, as in "we had to sack him, took too many sickies".

***Silly Buggers***: (a) to behave foolishly; (b) to waste someone's time. Does not imply homosexuality.

***Singlet***: sleeveless cotton undergarment mostly worn by men.

***Skippy***: (a) an Australian; (b) a kangaroo.

***Skint***: completely broke, no money at all (or none they will admit to having).

***Skite***: to brag immodestly about one's abilities or accomplishments.

***Sky Rocket***: rhyming slang for hip pocket.

***Skull***: to drink an entire glass of beer without pause.

***Slab***: a carton of beer containing 24 bottles or cans, as in "chuck us a slab of VB (Victoria Bitter)".

***Slacker***: a lazy person.

***Sleep-out***: a verandah enclosed and converted into a bedroom.

***Smash and Grab***: rhyming slang for cab.

***Smoko***: a short (10-15 min) rest break in the course of a working day, as in "I'm going out for smoko".

***Snag***: (a) a sausage; (b) a problem.

***Snow Job***: a confidence trick.

***Sook***: (a) a sulky person; (b) an overly sensitive person.

***Spag bol***: spaghetti Bolognese.

***Sparky***: electrician.

***Spewing***: (a) vomiting; (b) voicing one's anger.

***Spiffy***, looking good; especially for a special event.

***Spit the Dummy***: tantrum.

***Spot On***: (a) exactly right, (b) perfect.

***Spruiker***: (a) person outside an entertainment venue who entice people in with their sales-talk; (b) salesman on a radio or television advertisement.

***Sprung***: caught in the act of wrong-doing, as in "we sprung him with his fingers in the till".

***Spunky***: an attractive man or woman, as in "a girl's got to be spunky".

***Squizz***: (a) to examine; (b) to evaluate, as in "here, let's have a squiz".

***Standover Man***: enforcer for organised crime gang.

***Station***: (a) a substantial farm or sheep/cattle property; (b) transport depot.

***Stay Afloat***: rhyming slang for coat.

***Steak and Kidney***: rhyming slang for Sydney.

***Sticky-Beak***: a person who does not mind their own business.

***Stoked***: pleased, as in "I was stoked to win the surfing comp".

***Stone the (flamin') crows***: general purpose statement denoting a certain exasperation.

***Storm-Stick***: umbrella.

***Strewth, struth***: general purpose exclamation, derived from "God's truth", as in "Strewth son, so help me I'll wallop you from here till Tuesday if you don't stop!".

***Strides***: man's pants, jeans, trousers.

***Strine***: Australian English.

***Stubbie***: short necked (375ml) bottle of beer.

***Stubbies***: proprietary brand of men's hard-wearing shorts.

***Stuffed***: exhausted.

***Stunned Mullet***: blank, uncomprehending expression on a person's face, as in "she looked like a stunned mullet when I told her".

***Sucked-in***: duped.

***Sucked mango***: ugly or unattractive person, as in "he had a head on him like a sucked mango".

***Sunnies***: sun glasses.

***Surfers***: Surfer's Paradise, a holiday destination in Southern Queensland.

***Swag***: bedroll, usually carried slung across the back of itinerant workers and travellers.

***Swaggie***: swagman, a homeless itinerant worker or traveller, usually on foot.

***Swagman***: as swaggie.

***Sweets***: the desert course of a meal.

***Syphon the python***: to urinate.

# T

***TAB***: a government owned betting franchise, Totalisator Agency Board.

***Ta***: thanks.

***Tailgate***: drive so close to the vehicle ahead as to be somewhat dangerous.

***Take Away*** ...: food to be taken away to eat, rather than eaten on the premises.

***Tall Poppies***: high profile people. In Australia's egalitarian society, tall poppies are often "cut down" to size. This is known as the "Tall Poppy Syndrome".

***Tally Ho***: proprietary name for cigarette papers, for use in rolling one's own.

***Tart***: (a) a prostitute; (b) general derogatory term for a flashily dressed woman.

***Tee-Up***: make arrangements, as in "let's tee-up a meeting".

***Telly***: television, as in "do you do anything else besides sit on the couch and watch telly?".

***The Gabba***: cricket grounds at Wooloongabba in East Brisbane.

***Thingo***: watchamacallit, thingummy, whatsit, all general terms for items for which the proper name is either not known or cannot be recalled.

***Thongs***: rubber sandals, sometimes known as flip-flops.

***Thunder Box***: outside toilet, often little more than a hole in the ground, or a can with a seat above it.

***Tickets, to have on oneself***: to have an inflated sense of one's importance or capabilities.

***Tin Lid***: rhyming slang for kid.

***Tinnie***: (a) can of beer; (b) aluminium dingy often used by fishermen.

***Toey***: restless, as in "nothin' to do, feelin' a bit toey".

***Togs***: swim suit.

***Top End***: Far North of Australia

***Torch***: flashlight

***Trackie Dax***: track-suit or leisure-suit pants.

***Troppo***: a form of insanity caused by being too long in the tropics, as in "poor bugger's gone troppo".

***Trouble and Strife***: rhyming slang for wife.

***Trough Lolly***: small cake of slow-release deodorant placed in men's urinal.

***Truckie***: truck driver, especial of large articulated lorries and road trains.

***True Blue***: (a) genuinely Australian; (b) of undisputed loyalty.

***Tucker***: general purpose name for food, as in "yeah, but do we have any tucker?".

***Turps***: general name for poor quality alcoholic drink (derived from Turpentine originally but now including any kind), as in "he's been on the turps all week".

***Twit***: foolish person.

***Two-up***: a game of chance played by tossing two coins simultaneously and betting on the outcome, as in "he's in the back alley playing two-up".

***Tyke***: a young child, no longer a toddler, not yet at school.

# U

***U-ee***: a vehicular U turn, sometimes performed illegally, as in "he chucked a screaming u-ee at the lights".

***Ugg Boots***: loose-fitting sheep-skin slipper boots, originally from New Zealand.

***Underground Mutton***: rabbit.

***Undies***: underwear.

***Uni***: university.

***Unit***: a dwelling in a larger complex, as in flat, apartment, condominium.

***Up a Gum Tree***: stranded.

***Up Your-Self***: to have an inflated sense of one's importance or capabilities, as in "don't be so up yourself, you're no better than us".

***Ute***: a utility vehicle based for carrying loads, similar to a pick-up truck, as in "nice-looking ute".

# V

***VB***: Victoria Bitter, a brand of beer, as in "I paid him with a slab of VB".

***Vedgies***: vegetables.

***Vee Dub***: Volkswagen.

***Vedge Out***: to vegetate, usually on the couch watching TV, as in "What did you do on the holiday? Ah nothing much, just vedged out."

***Vegemite***: a salty sandwich spread made from rendered brewer's yeast.

***Vedjo***: vegetarian

***Vinnie's***: St. Vincent De Paul's Society, a charitable social welfare agency of the Roman Catholic Church.

# W

*WACA*: Western Australian Cricket Association, a legendary cricket ground in Perth, WA.

*Waggin School*: truancy from school, as in "missed you yesterday, didja wag it?"

*Walkabout*: (a) season migration or wandering by the indigenous folk; (b) any extended journey, especially one without a specific purpose.

*Walloper*: policeman.

*Waltzing Matilda*: (a) unofficial Australian national anthem, a song written by poet Banjo Patterson; (b) aimless wandering for the sake of wandering, especially in the bush.

*Wally*: a foolish, or accident-prone person.

*Wanker*: (a) one who pretends to be better than they are; (b) one who masturbates.

*Watchamacallit*: the name used for something when you cannot remember the actual name, as in "hey, can you pass me the ... umm watchamacallit there on the bench"

*Water Hole*: (a) a place to find a drink, especially an alcoholic one; (b) billabong, small lake, pond.

***Weekend Warrior***: Army reservist.

***Westie***: inhabitant of Sydney's western suburbs.

***Wharfie***: general term for a waterfront worker.

***Whadya know?***: general purpose conversation opener.

***Whinge*** – to complain, often about relatively trivial matters, as in "he's a shockin' whinger!".

***White Ants***: termites.

***White Pointer***: (a) a topless female sun-bather; (b) species of large shark found in Australian waters.

***Willy Nilly***: in a haphazard way.

***Willy Willy***: a small whirlwind, also known a dust-devil.

***Wino***: general term for someone who drinks cheap wine, often a homeless person (see "derro").

***Witchetty Grub***: a large edible insect larvae.

***Wobbly***: a temper tantrum, as in "he chucked a wobbly when he found out".

***Wog***: (a) general term for a cold or the flu; (b) derisive term for olive-skinned immigrants from the Mediterranean or Middle Eastern regions.

***Wombat***: Somebody that eats, roots & leaves (see also root) a simple minded person.

***Wooden god (dry as)***: desiccated, shrivelled through age.

***Woop Woop***: general name for a remote and unimportant place.

***Wowser***: a person who does not drink, and does not approve of others drinking either.

***Wuss***: a timid or cowardly person.

*XXXX*: Four X - beer of Queensland.

***Yabber***: speech, often garbled or otherwise nonsensical.

***Yabbie***: a small fresh water crayfish found throughout Australia in billabongs and waterholes.

***Yack***: to talk with others in an informal and amiable manner.

***Yakka***: physical labour, as in "digging that trench was hard yakka."

***Yank***: someone from the United States.

***Yarn***: a long and often complex narrative told by one person to another or a group.

***Yobbo***: a crude or uncultured person, often offensively so.

***Yonks***: a very long time, as in "jeez mate, haven't seen you in yonks."

***Young & Frisky***: rhyming slang for whisky.

***Young and Old***: rhyming slang for cold.

***Your Shout***: your turn to buy a round of drinks.

# Z

***Zack***: a sixpenny coin (pre-1966).

***Zane Grey***: rhyming slang for pay.

***Zebra Crossing***: pedestrian crossing.

***Zonked***: to be cognitively impaired, usually due to intoxication.

The End

# Afterword

Australia's unique and colourful history comes to life in its language. In the laconic Aussie drawl you can still hear the far-off accents of the early settlers. The Australian environment was and still is a very strange and often threatening experience for Europeans, at least for those who venture beyond the cities.

## *One-way trip to Botany Bay*

Britain in the $18^{th}$ Century had a problem; overcrowding in the cities, particularly London. With the overcrowding came crime. The authorities soon realised that there was a need to thin the population by removing the criminal under-class that had become established in the crowded working class areas of London and elsewhere.

Prison was a short-term solution, but these soon become impossibly over-crowded, so in desperation, the authorities resorted to using prison hulks, decommissioned ships that were no longer sea-worthy, but could nonetheless be anchored in the rivers and estuaries to house hundreds of prisoners. Conditions on these hulks were appalling, little better than slave transports.

Clearly a better, more permanent arrangement was necessary. The rational solution was to establish penal colonies in far-flung parts of the world. This had the added benefit of allowing Britain to claim ownership through right of occupation. These lands would eventually become valuable, income producing colonies.

In keeping with this strategy, the British established a penal colony in Botany Bay in what was to become Sydney in the 18th century. This location could hardly be more remote from England, which added to its attractiveness as a penal colony. Once a convict was brought to Australia, it would be almost impossible for him or her to escape and return to England. They could be considered permanently disposed of.

But it was not all bad. Convicts who behaved themselves and contributed to the building of a prosperous colony were rewarded in time with freedom and the right to own property.

## *Nearly French*

It is remarkable just how close it was that the country we now today as Australia was nearly a French colony. The French explorer Jean-Francois La Perouse came very close indeed to claiming *Terra Australis* for France. On 24 January 1788, La Perouse sailed into Botany Bay (to the south of Sydney Harbour, location of Sydney airport today) just as the Englishman, Captain Arthur Phillip was trying to move the new colony from there to Sydney Cove a few kilometres to the North in what is now called Sydney Harbour, close to the present-day site of the Opera House and Harbour Bridge.

Captain Phillip had arrived in Botany Bay only four days earlier on the 18th of January. There had been a strong on-shore wind blowing which prevented Phillip from leaving Botany Bay, while also preventing La Perouse from entering the Bay.

It is reported that the British received La Perouse and his officers courteously. Through interpreters, Phillip and La Perouse diplomatically discussed their situation and the situation was resolved amicably.

It is a matter of speculation that had the British not been there, Laperouse would almost certainly have claimed this superb, deep water harbour the name of France.

## *An Australian Republic*

At the time of writing (2013) Australia retains the British monarch as its ultimate head of state, a situation which many Australians find inappropriate, even absurd in the 21st century. The Governor-General of Australia is appointed by the British monarch on recommendation from the Australian Prime Minister. The Governor-General's role is ceremonial, signing-off on new legislation, swearing in government ministers, opening buildings and making speeches.

But the Governor-General has reserve powers that have been used in a highly political way in the past. On

November 11, 1975, the then Governor-General, Sir John Kerr used his power to dismiss the serving Prime Minister, Gough Whitlam. The dismissal precipitated a constitutional crisis and a general election. Whitlam's speech on the steps of Parliament House in Canberra on this infamous occasion summed up with typical orational flair the attitude of many Australians; *Well may we say "God save the Queen", because nothing will save the Governor-General!*

A concerted effort was made by the Republican movement in 2000 to bring about an Australian Republic in 2001, exactly one century after the Federation of the states was declared.

A referendum was held in and the monarchists won, partly because the then Prime Minister John Howard, an avowed monarchist, was able to frame the referendum question in such a way that a negative result was more likely, and secondly because there was disagreement among the republicans as to what republican model to use. One camp wanted a president to be directly elected by the Australian people, the other wanted a president to be appointed by the Prime Minister. More people wanted the former model, while the Prime Minister (John Howard) wanted the latter, saying that the President should not be a politician, as it would create a new political power-base to rival the Prime Minister. Constitutional experts agreed with Howard's view.

Little sentiment exists in 2013 to become a Republic. It seems likely that Australia will retain the British

Queen as its Head of State until Queen Elizabeth II serves out her term. .

# About the Author

David Tuffley is a fourth generation Australian. That makes him a "Dinki di Aussie". His Great Grandfather Henry Tuffley left the Leicestershire village of Hoby in the 1860's, to travel to far-off Australia on a dangerous sea voyage lasting several months. He eventually settled in Cooktown in Far North Queensland where he became a gold miner and somehow managed to live to a ripe old age.

David grew up on Brisbane's Southside in the working class suburb of Cannon Hill. As a child in the 1960's, he listened to the colourful speech of the old soldiers who had returned from World War II and the older soldiers who had served in WWI. Also listening to the stalwart wives and mothers who were the real glue of that society regardless of how irascible their men were. These men and women, now mostly gone, were the real repositories of Aussie Slang.

Become friends with David Tuffley on Facebook:

www.facebook.com/tuffley/

Made in the USA
Lexington, KY
30 June 2017